Discover Your Blueprint To A Fulfilling Lifestyle

NINE GUIDING TIPS FOR PERSONAL TRANSFORMATION

Salvatrice Cockrell

Overton Charm
PUBLISHING

Overton Charm Publishing

DISCOVER
YOUR BLUEPRINT TO A
FULFILLING LIFESTYLE

Contents

I Dedicate this book to **YOU**, because I truly believe that you are worthy, and I love you.

FULFILLED
Free your mind of negative thoughts and
Understand that you are worthy.
Love yourself no matter what you're going through.
Find the people and things that make you happy.
Identify your purpose.
Live every day to the fullest.
Lead by example and
Encourage others to believe in themselves.
Don't ever give up on yourself.

Disclaimer

Disclaimer:

The content provided in this book, including but not limited to text is for informational purposes only. The information in this book is not intended to serve as professional advice or replace talking with qualified professionals in the respective fields.

I **Encourage** you the reader to consult with appropriate professionals, such as licensed therapists, medical professionals, or financial advisors, before implementing any strategies or making significant decisions based on the content of this book.

The author and publisher of this book have made a sensible effort to ensure the authenticity and credibility of the information provided. The author and publisher of this book make no representations or warranties of any kind, express or implied, about the completeness, accuracy, reliability, suitability, or availability of the information contained herein.

The author and publisher deny any liability for injury, damage incurred, or any loss by readers as a result of the use or reliance on the information provided in this book. Readers are **100%** responsible for their interpretation and **Fulfillment** of the content presented.

The views and opinions expressed in this book are those of the author and do not necessarily reflect the views or opinions of any organizations or individuals mentioned herein.

By reading this book, readers acknowledge and agree to the terms of this disclaimer and accept full responsibility for their actions and decisions based on the information presented.

Introduction:

"The only limit to our realization of tomorrow will be our doubts of today."

— Franklin D. Roosevelt

Congratulations, by purchasing this book you are making it very clear that you are ready to discover "Discover Your Blueprint to a Fulfilling Lifestyle" which is a guide to start reclaiming control and rediscovering purpose in your journey. Life is a dynamic adventure filled with challenges, but with the right mindset and strategies, you can overcome obstacles and create a fulfilling life. In this book, we'll explore nine powerful principles to get back on track and establish a more fulfilling life. It will help you start to navigate the path to personal and financial success and happiness. As you work through this book you will be asked to do activities that will help you to gain a clearer vision of your future and better understanding of yourself. I ask that you do each activity to the best of your ability, this way you will get the most out of this experience. Trust me you won't be disappointed.

This book is for anybody who wants to get a better understanding of themselves, and to help you come up with ways to live a more fulfilled life. A more positive life does not mean you will not have any hard times because let me tell you, you will but you will have a clearer mind that will help you deal with those hard times a little better.

Please understand this will not be an overnight change you will have to continue to work on yourself day in and day out for the rest of your life, this book is just to help you get started. This end result is completely up to you. And I believe in you, and you can have a more fulfilling life that you desire.

Welcome to Your Journey

I would like you to take a little quiz to help give you a better understanding of what areas you will want to work on more in order to help get your life back on track. There are no right or wrong answers, but it is in your best interest to answer the questions as truthfully as possible.

Life Rehab Quiz: Assess Your Life Journey

For each question, choose the response that best reflects your current situation. Assign points based on the following scale:

- Yes: 2 points
- Sometimes: 1 point
- No: 0 points

Questions:

- 1.Do you have a clear vision of your short-term and long-term goals?
- 2. Are you actively working towards personal growth and self-improvement?
- 3. Do you have balance with your work and personal life?
- 4. Are you open to embracing challenges and viewing them as opportunities for growth?
- 5. Do you have a supportive network of friends, family, or mentors?
- 6. Is your daily routine designed to align with your goals and priorities?
- 7. Are you consistently breaking down barriers and overcoming obstacles?
- 8. Do you practice mindfulness or meditation regularly?
- 9. Have you identified and aligned your actions with your core values?
- 10. Are you actively pursuing your aspirations and passions?

- **0-10 points: In the Beginning**
  - You might be in the early stages of your transformation journey. Consider exploring the tasks in this book to gain clarity and direction in various aspects of your life.

- **11-15 points: On the Path to getting back on track**
  - You're making progress, but there's room for improvement. This score suggests you're on your way to transformation, and implementing additional strategies can enhance your journey.

- **16-20 points: On the right track**
  - Congratulations! Your high score indicates that you are actively engaged in the process of transformation. Keep building on your strengths and exploring new ways to elevate your life journey further.

My Agreement to Establish a more Fulfilling Lifestyle

I ____ am committed to doing the work in this book in order to create a more fulfilling lifestyle. I understand that I will not get the full experience by just reading the book. I commit to reflecting on my values and aspirations, actively working towards a well-defined vision for my life.

I recognize the importance of self-love in achieving holistic success. I commit to practicing self-compassion, embracing gratitude, and celebrating my unique qualities throughout my journey. I acknowledge that financial literacy is very vital to a successful life. I commit to mastering the basics of budgeting, saving, and investing. I understand that financial education is an ongoing process.

I acknowledge that my personal responsibility is the key to success. I commit to holding myself accountable for the actions and decisions outlined in this agreement. I am aware that this isn't an overnight fix and it will take time to get to where I truly want to be. I recognize the power of sharing my knowledge and inspiring others. I commit to sharing insights from The Blueprint to a Fulfilling Life with those who may benefit from its transformative wisdom.

By signing below, I affirm my commitment to the principles outlined in this book.

Signature:

____

Date: ___________________________________

I
―――――

Clarify Your Vision

"The only thing worse than being blind is having sight but no vision."
— Helen Keller-

The first principle to establishing a more fulfilling lifestyle that I would like to talk about is gaining clarity about your vision for the future. Define your goals, values, and aspirations. What does happiness look like for you? Let's start off with a life blueprint mapping activity, which will consist of you making a vision board. This activity will take some time so make sure you set aside an hour or so to focus. This isn't something that should be done quickly, it should be well thought out and make sure it's your own views and beliefs and not what you think someone else would want you to do.

Materials needed for this activity will be a large poster board or paper if you don't have the poster board, but the poster will give you a better layout. You will also need colored markers, pens, or pencils, Magazines, scissors, and glue. Now feel free to add whatever else you would like, be creative and remember this is your vision. I ask that you don't move forward with the book until you have completed this activity. If you do continue without finishing it that's ok but you will get more value if you complete this task first. I myself know how it is sometimes you just want to get to the meat of the information and do the activities later, but I promise you that taking the time to do each activity will give you a better overall experience on your journey through these six steps.

Activity: Life Blueprint Mapping

Now I want you to make your vision clearer by creating a Life Blueprint Map. A life blueprint map is what some might call a vision board, but I like to call it a life blueprint map because that's exactly what it is, a blueprint to where you want to go in life. This activity is designed to help you define your goals, values, and aspirations, providing a clear foundation for your vision.

Instructions:

- Find a quiet and comfortable space where you can focus without distractions.
- Divide the poster board into three sections: Goals, Values, and Aspirations.
- In the "Goals" section, Write down your short-term and long-term goals. Make sure you consider different aspects of your life, such as career, relationships, personal development, health, and more.
- Move to the "Values" section. Reflect on the core values that define who you are. Examples of core values could include honesty, integrity, family, creativity, and other principles that guide your decisions and actions.
- In the "Aspirations" section, I want you to create a vision board. Use magazines, scissors, and glue to create a visual representation of your aspirations. Look for images and words that resonate with the life you envision. Arrange and glue them onto this section of the board.
- Stop for a moment and look at what you have created. Are there any common themes or connections between your goals, values, and aspirations? Use colored markers to highlight key elements that stand out to you.

- Based on your reflections, write a concise vision statement that captures the essence of your clarified goals, values, and aspirations. This statement will serve as a guiding light on your journey.
- Now place your Life Blueprint Map in a prominent and visible location. This visual representation will serve as a daily reminder of your vision, helping you stay focused and motivated. I also want you to take a picture of it with your phone so that way when you are out you can still take a look at it and remain focused.

By doing the Life Blueprint Mapping activity, you actively define and visually represent the components of your vision, fostering a deep connection with your aspirations and providing a tangible guide for the chapters ahead.

Having a clearer vision of your future you can create a detailed roadmap for your journey that provides direction and purpose in your life. In order to understand your vision, you first must know what vision is, you need to know who you are and what is your purpose on this earth, then you want to create a mental picture of where you want to be in the future. Once you have those things figured out you are going to want to make sure you understand your values because that is what's going to guide you on your journey. The definition of vision is (the ability to think about or plan the future with imagination or wisdom). Your vision is like your compass to life, it will guide you along the way providing you with a sense of direction whenever you start to feel lost. Timothy Gallwey once said, **"If you have a clear vision of where you want to go, you are not as easily distracted by the many possibilities and agendas that otherwise divert you."**

Learning practical techniques for setting meaningful goals and aligning them with your core values helps make your journey through life a little easier. I want to give an example of core values just so we are on the same page, I know some people might not fully understand what core values are, so for instance my five core values are Self- respect, Knowledge, Integrity, Love, and Loyalty. I call it S.K.I.L.L. A few other core values would be humor, leadership, peace, and growth. But believe me there are many more. Take a moment and think of what you believe your core values are, there is no right or wrong answer to this, it's whatever you would like them to be. Once you know what they are, write them down and put them somewhere that you can see them every day. You might want to hang them on your fridge or put them in your wallet or purse to have with you at all times. There is nothing wrong with reminding yourself of who you are and what you stand for.

I want you to model your behavior after these values. So, for instance if one of your values is love, start to express more love to others each day, if one is in a growth mindset then start reading self-help books like: Think and Grow Rich by Napoleon Hill. Many things stuck out to me in the book but what really got me was how you can truly manifest your future. You do have to do the work though; I hope you did think it was that easy LOL. The book also helped me to believe in myself more and bet on me more. Another book I recommend is Jump: by Steve Harvey. Jump taught me that if you really want to be successful you have to be willing to Jump and take that risk. And to others would be the magic of thinking big by David Schwartz and Trash man to Cash man by Myron Golden. Now even though I gave you these four books there are so much more out there, don't limit yourself too just these. The more books you read the better off you will become.

Your journey is your journey so never compare it to someone else. We all have different core values and that's what makes the world so great, being yourself is much more powerful than you would think. People use many different techniques to create a more clarified vision.

> *"It's not hard to make decisions once you know what your VALUES are."*
>
> *-Roy E. Disney-*

II

A Growth Mindset

"When you go from a fixed mindset to a growth mindset, a new world of possibilities opens up."

-Imaan Farooq -

What is a growth mindset? Some may ask, Well I am glad you ask, so I tell you. A growth mindset is when people start to believe that their everyday abilities can be improved through dedication and hard work. It's time to shift your perspective from fixed mindset to growth-oriented mindset, viewing challenges as opportunities for learning and growth. Discover the power of resilience and how to bounce back from setbacks stronger than ever. This chapter will give you a few examples you can use in developing a positive mindset that fuels your journey toward a more fulfilling life.

Now there are many different ways you can develop a positive mindset but I will talk about one which helped me a great deal in my life, MEDITATION. Even when it comes to meditation there are many different styles which I will list in this chapter so you can choose which ones work best for you. We are all different so what works for me might not work for you and that's ok. When you first begin to practice meditation, I am going to tell you now it might feel a little funny at first.

Below is a list of a few different types of meditations and a brief description about how it they work:

- *Guided Visualization Meditation:*
  - Find a quiet space, close your eyes, and imagine vividly achieving your goals. A guided meditation recording or app can help direct your thoughts towards your vision, fostering clarity.
- *Mindfulness Meditation:*
  - Focus on your breath and bring your attention to the present moment. As thoughts arise, gently redirect your focus to your breath. This practice cultivates mindfulness, helping you gain clarity by quieting mental chatter.
- *Loving-Kindness Meditation:*
  - Extend feelings of love and compassion to yourself and others. This practice fosters positive emotions, creating a mindset that supports your vision and promotes clarity.
- **Body Scan Meditation:**
  - Pay attention to each part of your body, starting from your toes to the top of your head. This technique promotes relaxation and awareness, helping you identify physical and emotional aspects of your vision.
- *Affirmation Meditation:*
  - Repeat positive affirmations related to your vision. Affirmations help reprogram your subconscious mind, aligning your thoughts with your goals and creating a clear path forward.
- *Nature Meditation:*
  - Spend time in nature, either physically or through guided imagery. Connect with the elements around you, allowing the serenity of nature to inspire and clarify your vision.
- *Journaling Meditation:*

- ○ Combine meditation with journaling. After a few minutes of deep breathing or mindfulness, write down your thoughts, aspirations, and any insights that arise. This reflective practice aids in clarifying your vision.
- *Gratitude Meditation:*
  - ○ Reflect on the things you are grateful for in your life. Gratitude enhances a positive mindset, helping you see the possibilities and opportunities that align with your vision.

I want to let you know something about me, if you met me about 3 years ago I would have never said I believe you should meditate. A lot of people in the world think that meditation is a waste of time and I used to be one of those people, and you might be one of those people who feel that way and if you are I would like to ask you to trust me on this and try it out before you say it doesn't work. I ask you please don't quit, challenge yourself to do it for thirty days straight, if you do you will be amazed how at ease you will start to feel. Now this is going to take time because I am still working on mastering meditation but I can definitely say it has changed the way I look at life.

The more I did research and started to watch YouTube videos of people like Jim Rohn, Bob Proctor, Myron Golden and Dr Joe Dispenza just to name a few. These men have helped me change my mind set for the better and I am so thankful for coming across these gentlemen videos. Each of them has different styles of how you can cultivate a growth mindset but for me I was able to take a little from each and create my own way to change my way of thinking about myself and the world.

Watching Jim Rohn and Bob Proctor videos really helped me understand the law of attraction, I even watched the movie The Secret by Rhonda Byrne and Bob Proctor was the narrator for that movie and that's how I stumbled across him. From these two gentlemen I developed the understanding that my thoughts truly dictate my life outcome. I started to focus on the words I would use when I am speaking and what I would be thinking. For example, I might have said a line like: Oh, I cannot get that because I am broke or I can't get that because I don't have any money. Once I learned *"**Whether you think you can, or you think you can't- you're right"- Henry Ford-***

I started to use lines like: This cost this amount what can I do to get this item, or instead of saying I'm broke I would now say my money is a little slow. Now you might look at that and say that sounds crazy but for me I tricked my mind into believing yes, I can have that item, but it will just take some time. Before when I would say I'm broke I wouldn't even try to come up with a plan on how to get what I want. Myron Golden helped me develop a more spiritual approach on developing my growth mindset. He would use stories from the bible to help you relate to your everyday life, now I want to be clear yes, he uses the bible, but it is not in a religious aspect so even if you are not religious you can still get a great understanding of life from his teaching.

Dr Joe Dispenza in my opinion is like a combination of the three other men, he taught me how to train my mind so I can have a success-ful meditation experience as well as teaching how to be able to stay in a positive mindset even while you're not meditating.

Like I mentioned above, I have tried a few different meditation techniques. The ones that I found works well for me are guided visual-ization, Affirmation and Gratitude meditation. It is still a shock today how much meditation actually helps me. I truly see life in a more abun-dant and joyful way, and I love every moment of it. I hope that you can get the same out of it and more.

III

Setting Goals

"Setting goals is the first step in turning the invisible into the visible."

— Tony Robbins —

There are various approaches to measuring and setting goals, but I want to focus on creating S.M.A.R.T. goals. Your vision is the guiding force behind your actions, and well-defined goals provide the roadmap to turn that vision into reality. Just in case you aren't familiar with the term S.M.A.R.T. goal let me break it down for you. These are goals that should be Specific, Measurable, Achievable, Relevant and Time-bound. Now I want to mention that sometimes-setting goals for people can become a little discouraging, but I want you to understand that goal setting should make sense for what you are trying to achieve. What I mean by this is yes, the goal should be challenging but you don't want to make it challenging to where you don't even believe you can achieve it, unless it's a goal you plan on achieving in a few years or so.

But for your short-term goals that are maybe 2 years or less try to make it make sense. I hope that makes sense. Also, you don't want to make a goal that you know will be easy for you to achieve, I don't feel that goals like that would do you any favors. It doesn't drive you to put in the work (input) to receive the reward (output). You are like a farmer whose goal is to have a great harvest. In order to have a great harvest you must first plant good seeds (your ideas and work) and attend to your fields daily to make sure your seeds are watered and clear any weeds or insects that might damage our harvest. And in time you will have your harvest (achieving your goals). Now let's break down each part of the S.M.A.R.T goal.

Specific:

- You first want to make sure the goals are very clear and detailed; you can't leave any room for uncertainty. This makes it easier to plan and stay focused on actions. An example of a specific goal will be, I want to read at least two books per month and cut down on my social media time.

Activity: Goal Specification

- Breakdown your vision into specific goals. Ask yourself: What exactly do I want to achieve? Who will be involved? What resources do I need? What steps do I need to take to reach this goal?

Measurable:

- Now that you have the specifics next you want to make it measurable, so you will need to figure out a way to track your progress and measure success. This provides a tangible way to track your journey and allows you to be able to celebrate your achievements. Example of measurable is, I will read 50 pages a day and cut down my social media time by 20 minutes a week.

Activity: Establish Measurement Criteria

- Identify specific metrics or indicators to measure your progress. Consider how you will track success and when you'll know you've reached your goal.

Achievable:

- Your step in the goal setting process is to make sure your goal is achievable. I personally feel that this is one of the most important steps because like i mentioned before if you make a goal that's too hard to achieve you might get discouraged and give up. Make sure your goals are realistic and attainable for the resources and circumstances you have. I like to celebrate the small victories as I go, and you should too. I find that this keeps the motivation going.

Activity: Goal Achievable Assessment

- Evaluate whether your goals are realistically achievable within your current context. Adjust as needed to align with your capabilities.

Relevant:

- It is very important that your goals are aligned with your overall vision and are meaningful to your journey. Goals that are relevant will maintain focus and will minimize distractions from less impactful pursuits. For the goal of reading more it could be considered relevant to be able to learn more words to add to your daily vocabulary which allows you to become a better communicator.

Activity: Goal Relevance Check

- Assess whether each goal directly contributes to your vision. Remove or adjust goals that do not align with the overarching purpose.

Time-bound:

- The final step in the S.M.A.R.T process is time-bound, you are going to want to set specific timeframes and deadlines for each goal. Keep in mind if you don't complete your goal in the time you have set that does not mean you should stop, what you should do is reevaluate your goals and adjust the time and keep trying. Goals that are time-bound will create urgency and will cause you to facilitate effective planning.

Activity: Establish Timelines for Goals

- Assign realistic deadlines to each goal. Consider short-term and long-term timelines, ensuring they align with the overall vision.

These goals should be on your life blueprint map aka your vision board. If they aren't then you need to go back to your blueprint and add them. You are going to want to schedule regular reviews to assess your progress and make any necessary adjustments to your goals. Embrace the journey of growth and adaptation.

Clarity in your vision and the strategic setting of SMART goals are the foundation of a purpose-driven and successful journey. Take the time to effectively structure your goals and clearly express your vision. You will see your visions as a tangible and achievable destination and not just a dream that seems unreachable.

IV

Nurture Your Well-being

"Take care of your body. It's the only place you have to live."
— Jim Rohn

True success goes hand in hand with your well-being. Explore the importance of physical, mental, and emotional health in achieving your goals. This chapter provides guidance on adopting healthy habits, managing stress, and fostering a positive mindset. Discover the transformative impact of self-care on your overall well-being and success.

Activity: Well-being Assessment

Assess your current well-being by reflecting on your physical health, mental state, and emotional balance. Identify areas that require attention and improvement.

- I want you to rate your physical well-being on a scale of 1 to 10, 1 being poor health and 10 being great health. Then take a look at your eating habits and diet as well as your physical activity. Once you do that, create a plan on how to improve this area in your life.
- Your mental assessment: I want you to think about what you do to stimulate your mind and engagement. Are you challenging

your mind and stimulating your intellect with the activities you do? Are you working on things that help your personal growth and self-development? **Rate your overall sense of mental clarity on a scale of 1 to 10.**

- With the emotional part, take some time and really think about how you generally feel from day to day, are you happy, depressed, have a lot of anxiety or are you typically content? Point out what stresses you the most in your life. Then rate what you think your ability is to deal and cope with these emotions on a scale of 1 to 10.

I personally feel that this just might be the toughest one for many people to get accustomed to, the reason being is for many working out and eating healthy are not considered fun activities. I am definitely one of those people and I want to give credit here to those who love to do these two tasks or not necessarily love it but are consistent with it. I have always known that exercise and healthy eating is good for you, but it wasn't until I got older that I truly understood its importance. If we don't have our physical health, we cannot have anything else. I will not say I have mastered this part in life because I haven't, but I have definitely made major improvements and I continue to work on it one day at a time.

Let's start with physical health. I do want to state that I am not a doctor, personal trainer or nutritionist so everything I say about this topic is just my thoughts. I do recommend you speak with one of those professionals about the best way for you to get in shape and eat healthier. I don't expect anybody to just start off working out four to six days a week for like an hour a day. Absolutely not, if this is something you struggle with, I recommend you find an activity that's not so hard to do at first like walking twenty minutes a day and work your way up. Now for those of you who want to dive in and go hard from the jump, hey go for it. But remember if it starts to seem too hard not to quit completely just slow it down a little bit.

The goal is to become consistent in physical activity. We are not training for the Olympics. So, for me I used to be an athlete in high school, but I have never been one to enjoy working out, so now I work out at least a minimum of 3 days a week for twenty minutes a session. See I told you I am not a pro at this LOL. Now I know you might be saying that's not much but for someone who did not work out at all it is a step in the right direction. The most important part is to start.

If you can try to get a workout buddy so you can stay motivated, I would suggest someone who is already consistent with working out but if that's not possible then it's ok. I found out from personal experience and others that working out with people who hate it just as much as you can be unsuccessful. I say that because if I'm not motivated and my gym partner hits me up and says, " *Hey I don't feel like going today let's go out to eat instead." I would be like yea I don't feel like it either and before you know it we are paying for a membership that none of us is using. Have you ever experienced this or know someone who has? Now if you have someone who already goes to the gym on a regular basis and you tell them you don't feel like going, they going to be like "I get it but you can relax after this workout, see you soon." That right there is motivation because you don't want that person to look at you like you're lazy and not dedicated. If you don't know any regular gym goers then get you a personal trainer, ok I know PT costs money but it's important to invest in ourselves so start off with one who isn't so costly. If you are completely against the gym, I get that too, well you can always work out at home. You also have to make sure we get* sleep for optimal recovery and energy.

Take this journey one day at a time and don't worry about how long it will take to get consistent just keep working. If this isn't already enough to deal with, we have to incorporate healthy eating habits. Like I mentioned above, I am not a nutritionist so I will not give any recommendations on certain diets but what I will say is if you know you eat a lot of bad foods, like sugary and fatty foods, start cutting back one by one. Talk to a nutritionist and find out what's the best diet for you because we are all different. Start eating more fruits and veggies, and definitely drink more water than any other drink.

We just talked about physical health, now I want to talk a little about emotional health. Remember I am no professional I am just sharing my thoughts and things that worked for me and hopefully they can work for you. Like we talked about before, meditation and mindfulness exercises daily like deep breathing which people use to help relieve stress. You can find a lot of good videos to help with this on YouTube. These are a few good techniques to improve your emotional health. I also recommend taking a few breaks throughout the day when you feel you need to refocus. When you start to feel emotional, acknowledge the emotions in a healthy way. Look up different coping mechanisms that help with stress and setbacks. It is also very important to develop positive relationships that will provide emotional support.

V

Break Down Barriers

Break Down Barriers

"Obstacles don't have to stop you. If you run into a wall, don't turn around and give up. Figure out how to climb it, go through it, or work around it."
— Michael Jordan

Now I am going to ask you to do something that's going to be a little challenging and that is to identify and overcome the obstacles standing in your way. Whether they're internal doubts or external challenges they both must be dealt with before you can start to move towards a more fulfilling life. You will need to develop resilience and perseverance as you navigate through setbacks and learn how to turn challenges into steppingstones toward your goals. Life is a journey filled with challenges and obstacles. However, the ability to overcome these barriers is what defines our success. In this chapter, we will explore six effective strategies that will help you to break down barriers and turn your challenges into opportunities for growth and achievement.

Activity:

Take a few moments to reflect on your current doubts or uncertainties. We will call these barriers in your life. Write down 6 of them, three internal and three external and consider how addressing these doubts aligns with your desire for change.

Here are some examples of internal and external barriers:

INTERNAL BARRIERS	EXTERNAL BARRIERS
Self-Doubt	Financial Constraints
Procrastination	Lack of Resources
Perfectionism	Limited Support System
Lack of Self- Discipline	Workplace Barriers
Negative Self-Talk	Health Challenges

Your Internal Barriers

1. ____
2. ____
3. ____

Your External Barriers

1. ____
2. ____
3. ____

Take one of each internal and external barriers you identified above and create a detailed action plan. Break the barrier into smaller steps and outline specific actions you can take to address each step. I recommend these few steps to help you overcome these barriers.

The first step is to shift your mindset, so what I mean is instead of looking at these barriers as something stopping you, look at them more like hurdles in a track meet. With each hurdle you jump over there will be an opportunity to learn valuable lessons. You must have a positive mindset in order to overcome these barriers. You should practice affirmations to reinforce a positive mindset, challenge negative thoughts and replace them with empowering beliefs and focus on the lessons learned from challenges rather than dwelling on setbacks. These three tasks can definitely help you shift your mindset for the better. Remember like I said in the beginning of the book this isn't something that's going to be easy nor will you see a difference right away, self-development is a process. All I ask from you is to trust the process and keep working at it until it works no matter how long it takes.

The second step is to have strategies to overcome these barriers. A few examples of this would be:

Procrastination:

- *Description:* Delaying tasks due to a tendency to avoid or postpone.
- *Overcoming Strategy:* Break tasks into smaller, more manageable steps, set deadlines and stick to them.

Financial Constraints:

- *Description:* Limited resources or financial challenges.
- *Overcoming Strategy:* Create a budget, look into alternative funding sources, and seek financial advice on how to manage your money.

Step three would be to always look at your setbacks as learning experiences. You would want to work on developing a resilient mindset that helps you bounce back stronger after facing challenges. Take a moment to think of past challenges and acknowledge your ability to overcome them. How did you feel when you were able to overcome those challenges? Remind yourself that you have been overcoming challenges your whole life so these new ones will too soon be in the past. You may even want to seek guidance from people who have already overcome your current challenges, this can sometimes make it a little easier for you to face them yourself.

Step number four you are going to want to *develop practical problem-solving skills.* Analyze barriers objectively, identify potential solutions, and take decisive actions. Developing effective problem-solving skills empowers you to navigate obstacles efficiently. You are going to want to define the problem clearly and understand its root causes. Brainstorm multiple solutions and weigh their pros and cons and implement the chosen solution and adapt as necessary based on feedback.

Step five I want you to tell someone about your challenges. That someone could be a family member, a friend, a mentor, or someone people even would tell a social media group. We all need support on this journey we call life. Make sure whoever you tell is someone who will not judge you but will encourage you to keep going and will help you face your challenges. Seeking support not only provides emotional reassurance but also opens up opportunities for collaboration and guidance. You will find out by doing this not only does it help you but sometimes you could be helping the other person at the same time.

Step six is to embrace *change.* Be flexible in your approach and willing to adapt to new circumstances. The ability to pivot, when necessary, ensures that obstacles don't hinder your overall progress. One thing I know is that a lot of people have an issue with change at times, but I ask that you accept that change is a natural part of the journey. Adapting to unexpected change is an opportunity for growth and a learning experience. Stay open-minded and be willing to adjust your plans as needed.

Breaking down barriers is a continuous process that requires self-reflection and a commitment to personal development. As you implement these steps, regularly reflect on your progress and celebrate the milestones achieved.

Activity: Reflection Journal

Maintain a reflection journal to document your experiences in overcoming barriers. Note the lessons learned, personal growth, and how each obstacle transformed into an opportunity.

Breaking down barriers is not just about overcoming obstacles; it's about transforming challenges into steppingstones toward success. With a resilient mindset, strategic planning, and a supportive network, you have the power to conquer any barrier that stands in your way. Embrace the journey, learn from every experience, and let each obstacle propel you forward on your path to greatness.

VI

Recharge your Self-Love

"Love Always Wins, and that's the LAW."

-Myself-

We are going to explore the transformative process of recharging your self-love. Life's challenges and setbacks can sometimes put a damper on self-love, but it's never too late to reignite it. Discover the empowering strategies and practices that will guide you on the path to embracing and celebrating the incredible person you are.

In order to recharge your self-love, you must first understand it. The definition of self-love is; regard for one's own well-being and happiness (chiefly considered as a desirable rather than narcissistic characteristic). It is the practice of appreciating, accepting, and caring for oneself, as well as the foundation for a healthy and fulfilling life, influencing relationships, resilience, and overall well-being. You have to have self-compassion, by treating yourself with kindness and trying your best to understand your most difficult moments in your life. This will allow you to have a more positive inner dialogue about yourself as well as allows you to have more confidence when facing challenges.

Activity: Self-Compassion Practice

- Develop a self-compassion mantra or affirmation. Use it in moments of self-doubt or difficulty to cultivate a kinder and more supportive inner dialogue.

You must be mindful of self-reflection; you might be saying what does that mean? Well basically you are going to want to reflect on your thoughts, emotions and needs to get a better understanding of yourself. Write your thoughts and feelings in your journal. When you find yourself in challenging moments or negative self-talk use positive affirmations to reverse your thoughts about the situations. Use the self-compassion mantra to celebrate your strengths and potential. Repeat your mantra daily to reinforce a positive mindset. While you are on this self-love journey stop and give yourself gratitude, no matter if the accomplishments are big or small give gratitude. In your journal also document your positive aspects of your life.

So the same activities for your well-being can and should be used to recharge your self-love aka self-care. Make sure you have clear and healthy boundaries to protect your well-being and self-love. Remember to always acknowledge and celebrate your accomplishments. All the time.

Activity: Self-Love Action Plan

- Develop a personalized action plan incorporating the self-love strategies. Outline specific actions you will take daily, weekly, and monthly to rekindle and nurture self-love.

Recharging your self-love is a profound and ongoing journey that leads to a richer, more vibrant life. By embracing self-compassion, practicing gratitude, and celebrating your unique qualities, you pave the way for a renewed sense of self-worth and empowerment. Embrace this journey with an open heart and let the flame of self-love illuminate your path towards personal fulfillment and authenticity.

VII

Navigate Financial Literacy

"The number one problem in today's generation and economy is the lack of financial literacy."

Alan Greenspan-

Now I want to talk to you about financial literacy, but I must make a disclaimer again before we get into it. I am not a financial advisor. Yea I know you're getting tired of me saying that but I have to make sure you understand these are all just my opinions about things that helped me. This is just some basic information about financial literacy that I believe you would want to know. This also is not about how to get rich. If you have any questions about any of these topics, please reach out to your accountant or a financial advisor.

We will encounter the essential principles of financial literacy and I will give you a few strategies to help you control your financial situation. It doesn't matter if you are just starting out or already familiar and want to expand your financial knowledge, the journey to financial literacy is a necessary step toward achieving financial stability and future goals. First, we need to know what financial literacy actually is, financial literacy is the knowledge and understanding of financial concepts, such as budgeting, saving, investing, and debt management. Once you have a better understanding of it will allow you to make informed decisions about your finances, leading to greater financial security and independence. You will want to create a solid foundation and establishing a solid foundation involves mastering the basics of budgeting, saving, and understanding financial terminology.

Mastering basic budgeting is essential to having a strong financial foundation. All budgeting is to simply keep track of all your income (money coming in) and all your expenses (money going out). In the end if you have more money coming in then going out you're doing good, now unfortunately there are many people who spend more than they make and need to figure out how to get out of the financial hole they are in. To some this may seem impossible but with a little discipline and hard work it will all turn around.

When you get your budget in order you are going to want to make sure you put some money aside for an emergency fund, investing, savings for something big and for personal leisure. The emergency account should only be for just that, an emergency, for things like a new roof, in case you lose your job and things like that. Most people suggest you have at least three to six months of emergency savings. That is a good amount but with the way the economy is nowadays I say to work to have your emergency fund to cover at least seven months to a year of expenses (especially after the pandemic). Yes, it seems like a lot but you will get there in time just stay focused, you will be surprised at what you can do with dedication and hard work. Your emergency fund is different from your savings fund. Your future savings fund is for future purchases like buying a home, starting a business, education and things like that. Yes, I can hear you saying what about my personal things like vacations and stuff like that. Well, you will have another account for that. I will give you an example of how to break down your bills, you are free to adjust the numbers to fit your lifestyle. You can put aside ten percent of your income for each of these three savings. That's 30 percent of your total income, but you will fill these accounts after you take care of the other seventy percent of your earnings.

The seventy percent will be for your bills, mortgage/rent, car payment, insurance, utilities, phone, and transportation (gas and car maintenance.). This would probably be about thirty percent to forty depending on how high your expenses are. About ten percent at least to investments but if you can put more that's great. The rest you can use for your everyday living and to buy things that aren't needs but wants. But I would suggest that you don't spend all on wants, try to add more to your investment accounts instead and just a little on wants. This isn't a fun approach, but it will allow you to have more fun in the future. Last but not least you will want to give ten percent to tithing or charity, some people don't agree with this one but i feel it's the most important, but I say it truly is. Winston Churchill once said, "We make a living by what we get, but we make a life by what we give." Here is the breakdown in numbers for you so you can have a better picture of what I am saying, remember you can adjust as you see fit:

- Household needs (mortgage/rent, insurance etc.)...........30%
- Pay yourself for fun activities:................................20%
- Investments (real estate, stocks etc.)...................10%
- Personal savings (vacations etc.)........................10%
- Emergency fund..10%
- Savings (buying a home, starting a business)....................10%
- Tithe/Charity.. 10%

Total   100%

Activity: Create a Basic Budget

- Develop a simple budget that outlines your income, expenses, and savings goals. This foundational step lays the groundwork for effective financial planning.

Here is a copy of a monthly budget I made, feel free to modify the template based on your specific financial situation and goals. Here is the QR code below, you can use this one or any other budget template you choose. When you open the link, you will want to make a copy of the template so you can use it:

You also must understand credit, credit plays a crucial role in financial health. Understanding the basics of credit scores, reports, and responsible credit use is very important. Obtain a free copy of your credit report, review it for accuracy, make sure everything up there belongs to you. Familiarize yourself with factors that influence your credit score like credit card utilization credit history and diversification to name a few. Credit card utilization is the percentage you use of your credit card. For example, if you have a $5000 credit limit and you used $2500 that would mean you are at 50% utilization, you are going to want to try to keep your utilization around 15%. To diversify your credit, you might have like one or two credit cards which could be a revolving credit and then maybe a personal loan, car loan or mortgage these would be called installment loans. Your credit history is just what it sounds like how you handle your credit over a period of time. You will want to make payments on time and only use your credit cards when you have the money to pay it off, unless it is an emergency.

Even though I am telling you all this you still need to do your own research and understand it yourself. It doesn't matter if your credit score is 350 or 850 you still want to check your report every year to make sure everything is accurate. Debt can be good debt or bad, good debt would be like a house and bad debt would be like having high credit card balances. If you have a lot of debt you will want to create a repayment plan for those accounts. One way you can lower your debt is to use your repayment plan strategy and pay off the high-interest debts first. Once again do your own research to see what other ways you can reduce your debt, there are many different ones out there.

Another part of financial literacy you will want to learn at least the basics to would be investing. Hopefully you already know something about the market but if not please be willing to learn. Yes, the market is very complex, but I just recommend you learn enough to invest for the future. Now if you want to learn how to be a day trader or trading options and forex by all means go for it. The more you are willing to learn the better off you will be in the long run. What are stocks? Well stocks, or shares, represent ownership in a company. When you own a stock, you own a portion of that company and its assets. I will explain the different types of stocks. Common stock which gives its shareholders voting rights in the company decisions, then you have preferred stocks which provide a fixed dividend but usually no voting rights. Just in case you don't know, a dividend is an amount of money paid typically quarterly to shareholders out of the company's profit. There are also what's called blue-chip stocks, these stocks represent shares in large, well-established companies with a history of stability. Examples of a blue-chip stock would be companies like Apple, Bank of America and Berkshire Hathaway. There are many more components when it comes to trading and investing.

It is very important to understand that all investments carry some level of risk. Understanding and managing risk is crucial. Balancing risk and reward are key to building a resilient and successful investment strategy. This is not something I recommend you just jump into head-first without doing yup you guessed it LOL any research the market is not like the casino you don't want to gamble you want to make educational discussions. Staying up to date on what's happening in the world is a great way to stay on top of the stock market. The market is dynamic, influenced by economic events, company news, and global trends.

By understanding the basics, building a diversified portfolio, and actively managing risks, you position yourself for a rewarding experience in the world of stocks. Remember, patience and continuous learning are the keys to long-term success in the ever-evolving landscape of stock investing

Activity: Stock Research

- Research and create a list of companies you're interested in. Understand their business models, financial health, and market performance. Talk to someone who is a professional in the field and see if the stocks you picked are good to invest in. Once you do that, open an account and make your first investment for the future.

VIII

Build a Support System

"Surround yourself with only people who are going to lift you higher."
— Oprah Winfrey

No journey is meant to be traveled alone. Cultivate a strong support system that encourages and uplifts you. Your support system is what I like to call your team of life. Learn how to communicate effectively, seek help when needed, and surround yourself with positive influences. Let's explore the power of collaboration and connection, emphasizing the importance of community in achieving and sustaining success. Together, we'll discover the transformative impact a strong support system can have on breaking down barriers and achieving your goals.

A support system is a collection of different people in your life. It can be a makeup of any of your friends, mentors, colleagues and family members who help contribute to your well-being and personal growth. A support system is also a network of individuals who provide encouragement, guidance, and assistance during various aspects of your life.

Even though they will be your support system you just might be a part of theirs as well. So take as much feedback from them as you can but remember you should offer them support when needed in return.

"

Activity: Support System Reflection

- Take a moment to reflect on your current support system. Identify individuals who have been instrumental in your personal and professional development. Consider the qualities and types of support they provide. Now if you say to yourself, I don't have a support group, I would like for you to take the time to think of about five people who you can become your support group and go from there.

List of possible people to be in your support system:

____

____

____

____

____

Building a support system is a cornerstone of personal and professional success. In this chapter, we explore the importance of surrounding yourself with a network of individuals who uplift, inspire, and propel you forward on your journey. Together, we'll discover the transformative impact a strong support system can have on breaking down barriers and achieving your goals.

In order to build an effective support system, you first must understand some important elements that are needed. You need to have positive encouragement, which will be individuals who give uplifting words and positive reinforcement. This is important because it will boost your confidence, give you motivation when you don't feel like doing a task and will help you become resilient in the face of challenges. You will also need to find an experienced individual who can provide you guidance and mentorship. Mentors give valuable advice and insight on where you are going in life, a great mentor will help speed up your learning curve and give you wisdom on challenges you will face. There is a saying by Roy H Williams *"A smart man makes a mistake, learns from it, and never makes that mistake again. But a wise man finds a smart man and learns from him to avoid the mistakes all together." You are going to need someone on your team for emotional support.*

They will offer empathy and understanding when you are facing hard times. Emotional support gives us a sense of belonging and helps build up your mental and emotional resilience. You will also need accountability partners. This individual will hold you accountable for your goals and actions, they will provide discipline and ensure that you stay focused on your task and don't get too far off track. I would also recommend you join some type of collaborative networking group. These groups provide diverse perspectives, potential partnerships and resources. They can be online groups, but I feel you will get a better experience from in person networking groups.

So, you have some of the elements for a strong support system (team of life). Now let's look at some strategies for building the support system. The people you choose should be aligned with your current needs and goals. If you want to start your own business, it will be best for you to find someone who is successful at running their own business or has previously run a successful business to be your mentor for that topic. You would not want someone who doesn't know anything about business because how can they guide you to where you are trying to go? You might look at the elements and say you can have one person take on more than one role and that's true, but you will get a better experience by diversifying your network.

This will give you different views on how to do things and will allow you to see life from different angles. In order for this system to work for you, you have to communicate your goals, challenges, and expectations as clearly as possible to them. This will build trust and give them a better understanding of your vision. The most important thing you can do for your support system is to show gratitude and acknowledge their contributions and celebrate your success with them. You will also want to give your support and encouragement to them as well, this will strengthen the relationship of the entire support system.

A successful support system is not just a safety net; it is motivation for personal and professional achievement. Welcome the connections around you, encourage meaningful relationships, and watch the collective power that moves you toward your aspirations. Keep in mind that you are going to want to regularly examine the effectiveness of the team, look for areas that may need improvements and you must be willing to make the proper adjustments for evolving relationships as you grow and pursue new goals. In the journey of life, your team of life you build becomes a vital companion, sharing in the achievements and navigating the challenges alongside you.

IX

Design Your Ideal Routine

"When you want to succeed as badly as you want to breathe, then you'll
be successful."
- Eric Thomas-

Create a daily routine that supports your goals and priorities. Learn effective time management strategies, prioritize tasks, and eliminate distractions. A well-designed routine enhances productivity, reduces stress, and helps you stay focused on what matters most. This chapter provides practical tips to design a routine that aligns with your vision and promotes a balanced and fulfilling life.

So, I am going to give you a routine example. You can either use this exact one or alter it so it best fits your life schedule. We all have different lives, and I don't expect us all to be on the same schedule. That would be insane. Also do not feel you have to have everything in your schedule that i list but i would say try to at least have half if possible and they can be in your own order.

We will start off with the morning ritual: this will consist of waking up early for a calm start by practicing mindfulness and/or meditation for about 15 minutes, feel free to go longer. Then review and visualize your goals for the day. I would say this would be around the hours of 6 am to about 7:30 am. If you wake up earlier or later that is fine as well.

From 7:30 am to about 8:30 fit in some exercise (e.g., jogging, yoga, or strength training). If you have time, fit in a healthy breakfast so you can have energy to start your day. It doesn't matter if you are working at a job, self-employed or not currently working, you still should use the hours from 9 am to about 1 pm to focus on high-priority tasks during peak productivity hours. During this time, you would want to take short breaks to maintain energy and so you don't lose your concentration.

When it is lunchtime, set time aside to practice a brief mindfulness exercise to recharge. Also try to eat something healthy, now i know this can be challenging to eat healthy all the time but do the best you can and as times goes on it will get easier. After lunch between the hours of 2 pm and 5 pm you will finish up your work for the day if you work longer hours that is fine also. Once you are done with work it is very important to spend quality time with family or engage in personal hobbies. During this time, you most likely would have dinner as well at dinner its important to unplug from technology as much as possible. You should be present in the moment, once you are done with dinner you should go over your day's achievements and areas for improvement. This would bring you to around 8 pm to 9 pm and now you would want to get ready to unwind by engaging in a calming activity (reading, listening to music, or a warm bath). Now it about time to go to bed but before you do you should practice a brief relaxation or gratitude exercise. Then you do it all over again the next day.

STEP 1: TIME AUDIT

Before crafting your ideal schedule, it's essential to understand how you currently spend your time. The Time Audit will help you identify areas for improvement and optimization.

Activity: Time Audit

- *Record Your Activities:*
  - Keep a detailed log of your activities for a week. Note the start and end times of each task, including work, leisure, and sleep.
- *Categorize Activities:*
  - Categorize each activity into segments such as work, personal development, family time, relaxation, and sleep.
- *Identify Time Drains:*
  - Highlight activities that consume significant time without contributing to your well-being or goals.
- *Assess Productivity Peaks:*
  - Identify periods of the day when you are most productive and focused.
- *Reflect on Energy Levels:*
  - Note your energy levels throughout the day. When do you feel most energized, and when do you experience dips in energy?

STEP 2: SCHEDULE DESIGN

Now that you have insights from your Time Audit, it's time to craft a schedule that optimally utilizes your time and energy.

Activity: Schedule Design

- *Define Your Priorities*:
    - Clearly outline your short-term and long-term goals. What activities contribute most to these goals?
- *Allocate Time for Peak Productivity:*
    - Place high-priority tasks during periods when your energy and focus are at their peak.
- *Balanced Work and Breaks:*
    - Schedule regular breaks to maintain focus and prevent burnout. Use techniques like the Pomodoro Technique (work for 25 minutes, then take a 5-minute break).
- *Incorporate Personal Development:*
    - Dedicate time to activities that contribute to your personal and professional growth, such as learning, skill development, or reading.
- *Prioritize Self-Care:*
    - Allocate time for self-care activities, including exercise, mindfulness, and relaxation.
- *Quality Family and Social Time:*
    - Schedule dedicated time for family and social connections. These moments contribute significantly to your overall well-being.
- *Optimize Sleep Routine:*
    - Ensure sufficient and consistent sleep by setting a regular bedtime and wake-up time. Prioritize sleep as a non-negotiable aspect of your routine.
- *Flexibility for Spontaneity:*

Allow flexibility in your schedule for unexpected events or spontaneous activities. A rigid routine may lead to stress if things don't go as planned.

STEP 3: IMPLEMENTATION & DESIGN

Put your designed schedule into action and consistently follow it. Regularly assess its effectiveness and make adjustments as needed.

Activity: Weekly Review and Adjustment

- *Weekly Review:*
  - Reflect on the past week. Did the schedule align with your goals and priorities? Identify any challenges or adjustments needed.
- *Adjustments for Optimization:*
  - Based on your reflections, make adjustments to the schedule. This could involve shifting tasks, optimizing break times, or reallocating time based on changing priorities.
- *Celebrate Successes:*
  - Acknowledge and celebrate achievements and positive changes resulting from your new schedule.
    Your ideal schedule is a living document that evolves with your goals and life circumstances. Continuously refine and adjust it to ensure it remains a supportive framework for your journey toward success and well-being.
    "The secret of your future is hidden in your daily routine."
    - Mike Murdock -

X

Resolution:

"Do the best you can until you know better. Then when you know better, do better."
— Maya Angelou–

"Discover Your Blueprint to a Fulfilling Lifestyle" is your guide to regaining control, overcoming challenges, and creating a life that lines up with your ambitions to achieve your desires. By incorporating these nine strategies, you'll not only start to get your life back on track but also start on a transformative journey toward a more purposeful and fulfilling living. Embrace the adventure, and let your new way of living unfold, success is an ongoing process, fueled by courage and persistence. When it comes to breaking down barriers is not just about overcoming obstacles; it's about transforming challenges into stepping-stones toward success. Keep a clear mindset, use strategic planning, and utilizing your supportive network, you will have the power to overcome any barrier that stands in your way. Every barrier is a learning experience and let each of them help you to move forward on your path of fulfillment.

I want you to understand your journey is not a linear path but a dynamic voyage of self-discovery and growth. Clarify your vision, nurture self-love, and embrace financial empowerment as interconnected elements guiding you toward a life of purpose, resilience, and fulfillment. You must recognize that challenges are opportunities for growth, and setbacks are steppingstones toward your aspirations. With each chapter, you've equipped yourself with valuable tools, insights, and activities to empower your personal and financial well-being.

By mastering the basics of budgeting, saving, and investing, you lay the foundation for a more secure and fulfilling financial future. Embrace this with curiosity and commitment, knowing that each step brings you closer to living life on your terms.

Stock investing is an exciting step toward financial growth. By understanding the basics, building a diversified portfolio, and actively managing risks, you position yourself for a rewarding experience in the world of stocks. Remember I am not telling you to become an expert in investing, but it is important to at least learn enough to where you can invest and make money. Let's not go in this blindsided. patience and continuous learning are the keys to long-term success in the exciting world of stock investing.

Embrace the continuous journey of self-improvement, and may your path be marked by resilience, self-love, and the fulfillment of your unique vision for success. I want to encourage you to do your research on each of these principles so you can find different techniques that can also help you on your way to a more fulfilling life. **I BELIEVE IN YOU!!!**

Examples of Affirmations

I am successful

I am a winner

I deserve respect

I am FULFILLED

I am stronger than I know

I am grateful for every moment of my life

I am confident

I am unbreakable

I am powerful

I deserve the best

I am a leader

I will trust the process

Fulfilling Thoughts

About the Author

Salvatrice Cockrell grew up in a small town called Middletown, Connecticut. She lived with her mother Ruby and her older brother Charles. Salvatrice or Salva (which is what everyone calls her by the way) grew up battling different obstacles and had a very negative outlook on life. She had fallen out of a 2-story window at the age of 4, got into a car accident and had to learn how to walk again at the age of 22, and a many other life changing events. But She would tell you all of those things has helped her transform her life. If these things didn't happen, you wouldn't be able to get the experience that this book has to offer. Once she transformed her way of thinking she was able to discover her blueprint to start living a more fulfilling life, just as she wants for YOU.